My first handwriting book

About this book
This book is for children who need to learn how to write in English. It can be used by parents at home with their children and by teachers with their classes. In this, the first of two books, the children learn how to print all the lower case and capital letters from left to right. They also learn how to write numbers.

Before you begin
1 Make sure that your child or pupil is sitting comfortably. The chair should be at a suitable height for the desk or table at which the child is writing.
2 For right-handed children the paper or book should be to the right of an imaginary line running through the centre of the body. For left-handed children it should be to the left. The paper or book can be slanted as shown in the diagram below.

Left-handed child   Right-handed child

3 Use the type of pen or pencil that is most comfortable for your child.
4 Make sure that your child is holding the pen or pencil correctly. The following illustration shows the best position for writing. The grip should be firm, but not too tight.

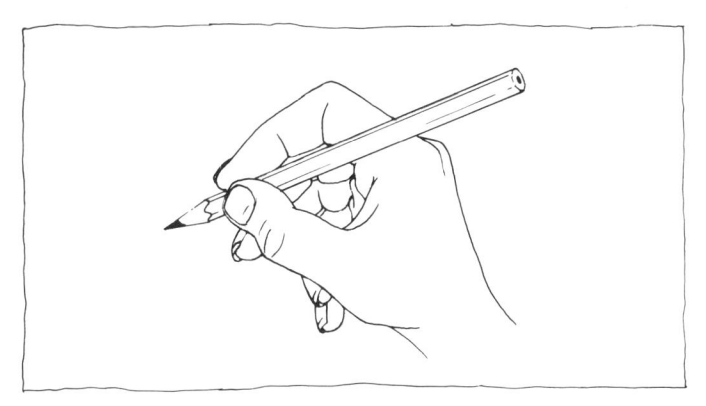

Before you begin to use this book, draw some of the patterns below on the board or on a piece of paper for your child to copy from left to right. See how your child is holding the pen or pencil whilst copying the patterns. Modify the grip if it looks awkward.

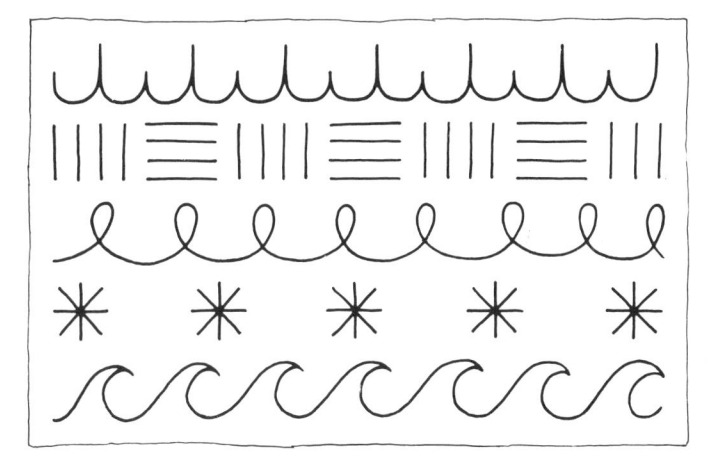

5 Some children are naturally left-handed. Some of the cleverest people in history were left-handed: Einstein was, and so was Leonardo da Vinci. Never try to force a left-handed child to use his or her right hand as it could create very serious learning difficulties. Here are some ways in which you can help left-handed children.

- The important thing to remember is that left-handed children push their pencils, they do not pull them. Make sure that the paper or book on which they are writing is in the best position and that they are not impeded by children sitting next to them.

1

- Watch out for natural left-handers who try to write like their more numerous right-handed friends. Even though you do not force them to 'be the same as everybody else', some left-handers try to adopt a pulling style of writing by an 'over the top' grip. This grip usually makes it difficult to write legibly and quickly. Help children who develop the habit to adopt a more comfortable left-handed style.

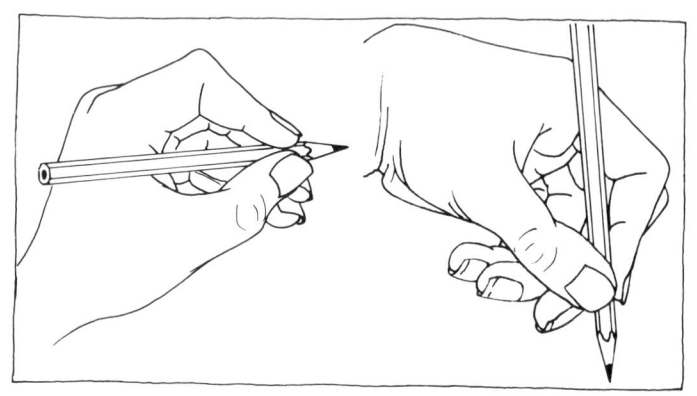

Good grip   Bad grip

How to use this book

There are three main teaching steps in this book for each lower case letter. There are also odd one out and letter matching exercises. The following is a list of the steps, their aims, and how to teach them.

1 Finish the picture

Aim: to practise the overall shape of a family of letters using pictures. (Letter families are groups of letters which have similar shapes.)

- Draw the picture on the board or on a piece of paper. Explain what you are doing. Say, for example, 'Start at the bottom and go up. Draw from left to right'.
- Practise tracing the shape of the letter in the air. Stand with your back to your child or class and get them to imitate your movements as you trace the shape in the air. Next, stand behind them and tell them to trace the shape. You will be able to see if they are making mistakes from this position.
- Practise tracing the letter shapes in the book using the blunt end of the pencil. Tell the children to complete the picture, using the solid model as a guide. Make sure that they are moving from left to right.

2 Trace the letters

Aim: to practise tracing the shape of lower case letters which are slightly larger than normal. Begin with the first letter.

- Show the children how to trace the shape of the first letter using the blunt end of the pencil. Explain that they must begin at the dot and follow the numbered arrows.
- Let the children practise doing this on their own a number of times. Watch them carefully to make sure that they follow the shape of the letter correctly.

3 Copy the letters

Aim: to practise tracing and writing the lower case letter.

- Draw four parallel lines on the board and show the children how to write the letter. Tell them what to do as you do it. Say, for example, 'Start at the top and go down. Then go up and round and down'.
- The children then practise tracing the letters on the top row of the exercise. They then go on to copy the letters, from left to right, on the lines underneath. Make sure that they use the black line as their base line and write correctly between the other lines.
- If children have problems with any of the letters, give them extra practice by drawing four line staves in their exercise books and writing the letter for them to trace and copy.

When you have completed these three steps for the first letter on the page, repeat them for the second letter.

4 Odd one out and letter matching exercises

These are testing exercises for reading in which the children identify odd or matching letters from a group with similar shapes. This is an important exercise because some letters are only slightly different from others. Consider *b* and *d* which are the same except that the curve is on the left in *d* and on the right in *b*.

- Demonstrate the exercise on the board or on a piece of paper.
- The children draw circles round the odd or matching letters.

There are also three main teaching steps for each upper case letter. The following is a list of the steps, their aims, and how to teach them.

1 Trace the letters

Aim: to practise tracing the shape of upper case letters which are slightly larger than normal.

- Teach this step in the same way as Step 2 for lower case letters.

2 Copy the letters

Aim: to practise tracing upper case letters.

- Draw four parallel lines on the board and show your children how to write the letter.
- The children then practise tracing and copying the letter.

3 Practise the letters

Aim: to practise tracing and writing each upper case letter with its lower case version.

- Revise the correct formation of each lower case letter.
- Write the upper and lower case of each letter on the board.
- The children practise tracing and copying the letters on the top row of the exercise. They then copy the letters on the lines below.

1 Follow the arrows.

1 | Finish the picture.

2 | Trace the letters.

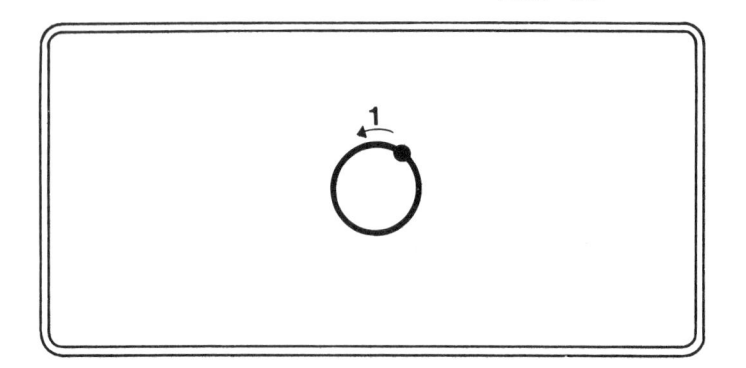

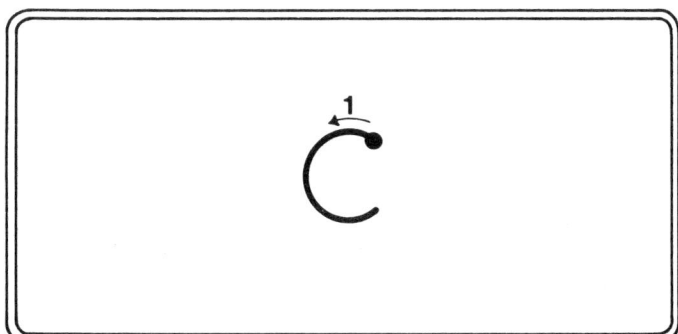

3 | Copy the letters.

1 Finish the pictures.

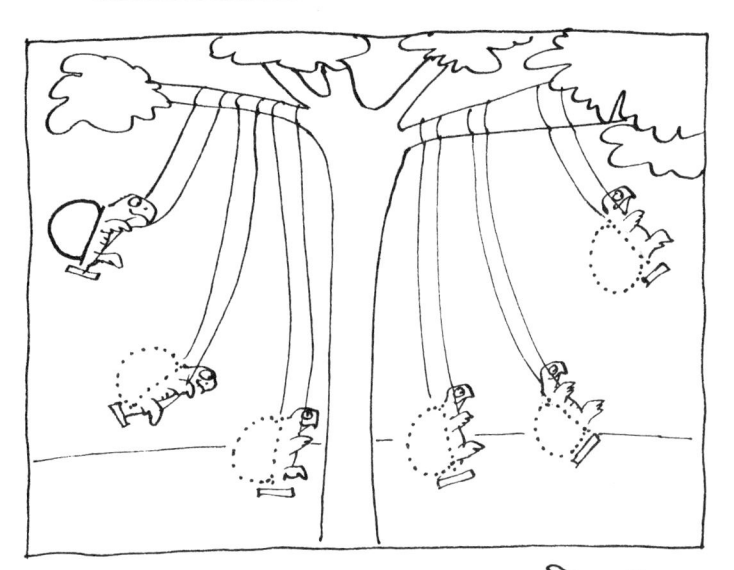

2 Trace the letters.

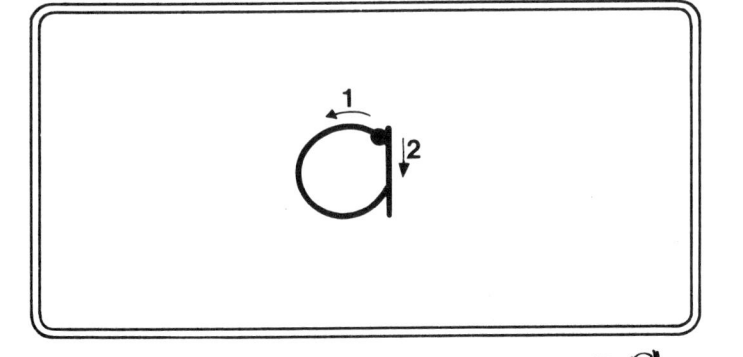

3 Copy the letters.

a a a a a a a a   e e e e e e e e

1. Finish the pictures.

2. Trace the letters.

3. Copy the letters.

s s s s s s s s

d d d d d d d d

1 Finish the pictures.

2 Trace the letters.

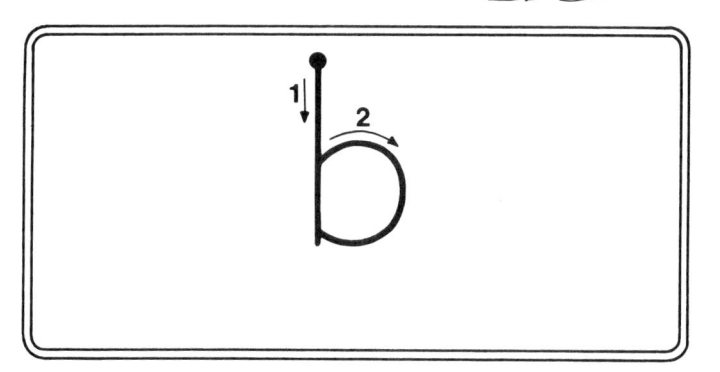

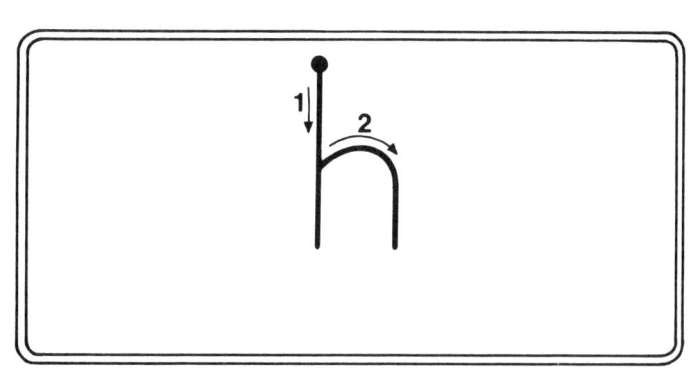

3 Copy the letters.

1 Finish the pictures.

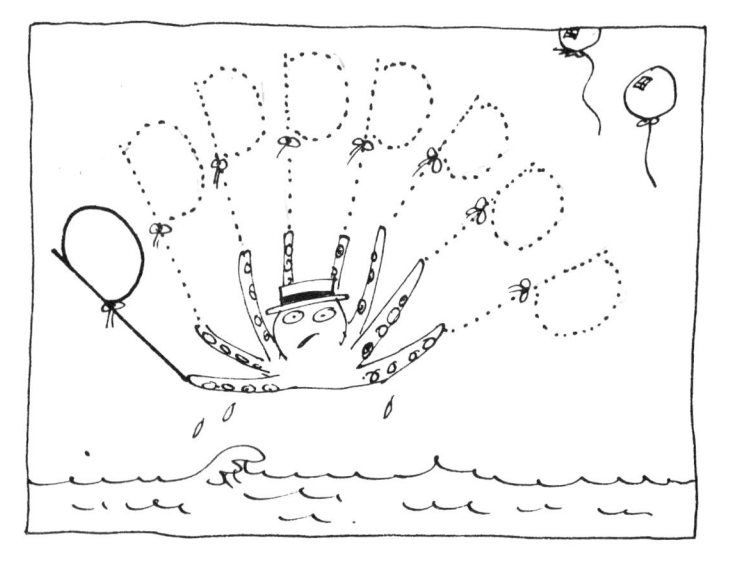

2 Trace the letters.

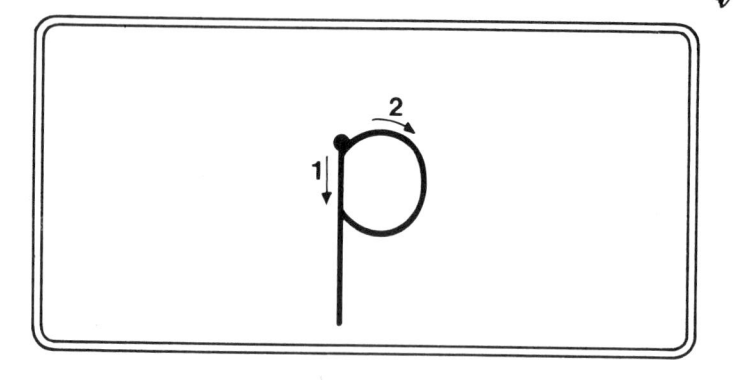

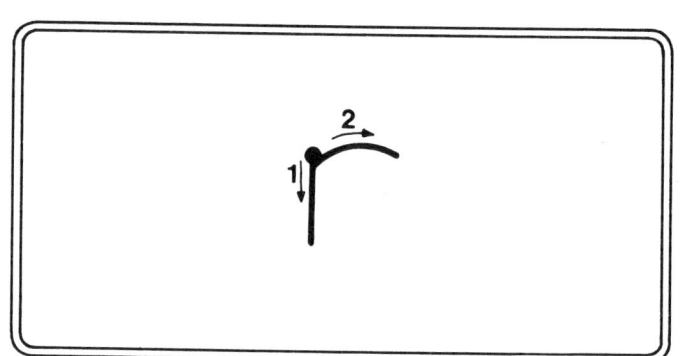

3 Copy the letters.

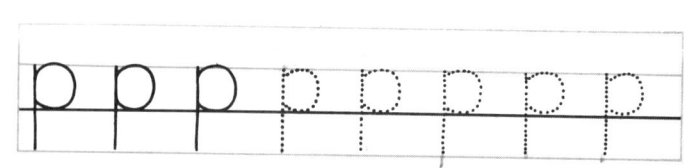

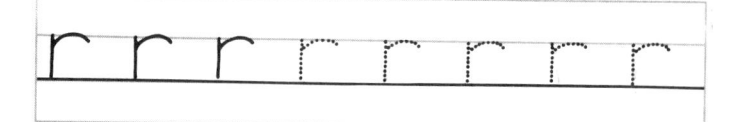

1 Finish the picture.

2 Trace the letters.

3 Copy the letters.

1 Finish the picture.

2 Trace the letters.

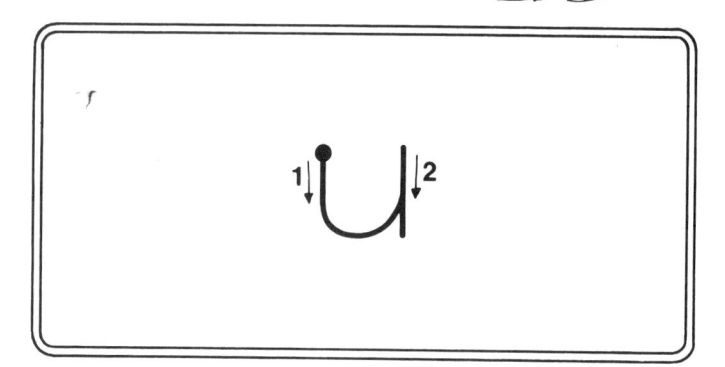

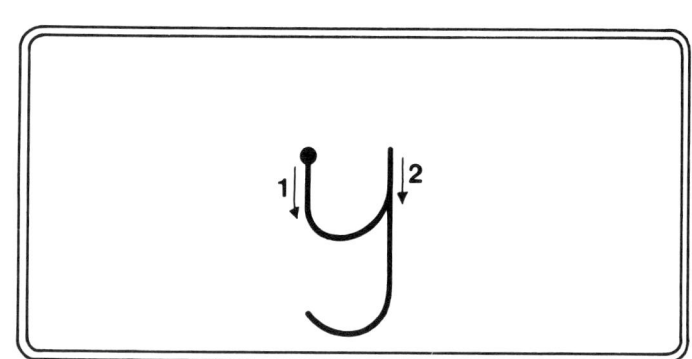

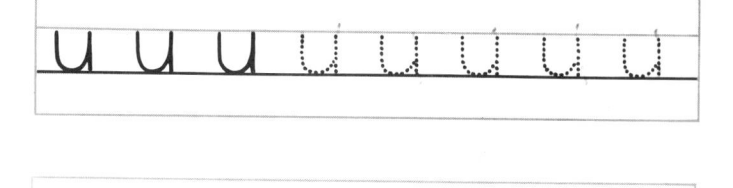

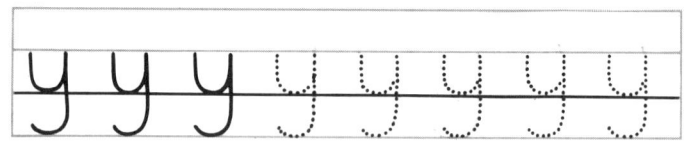

u   y

3 Copy the letters.

u u u u u u u u   y y y y y y y y

10

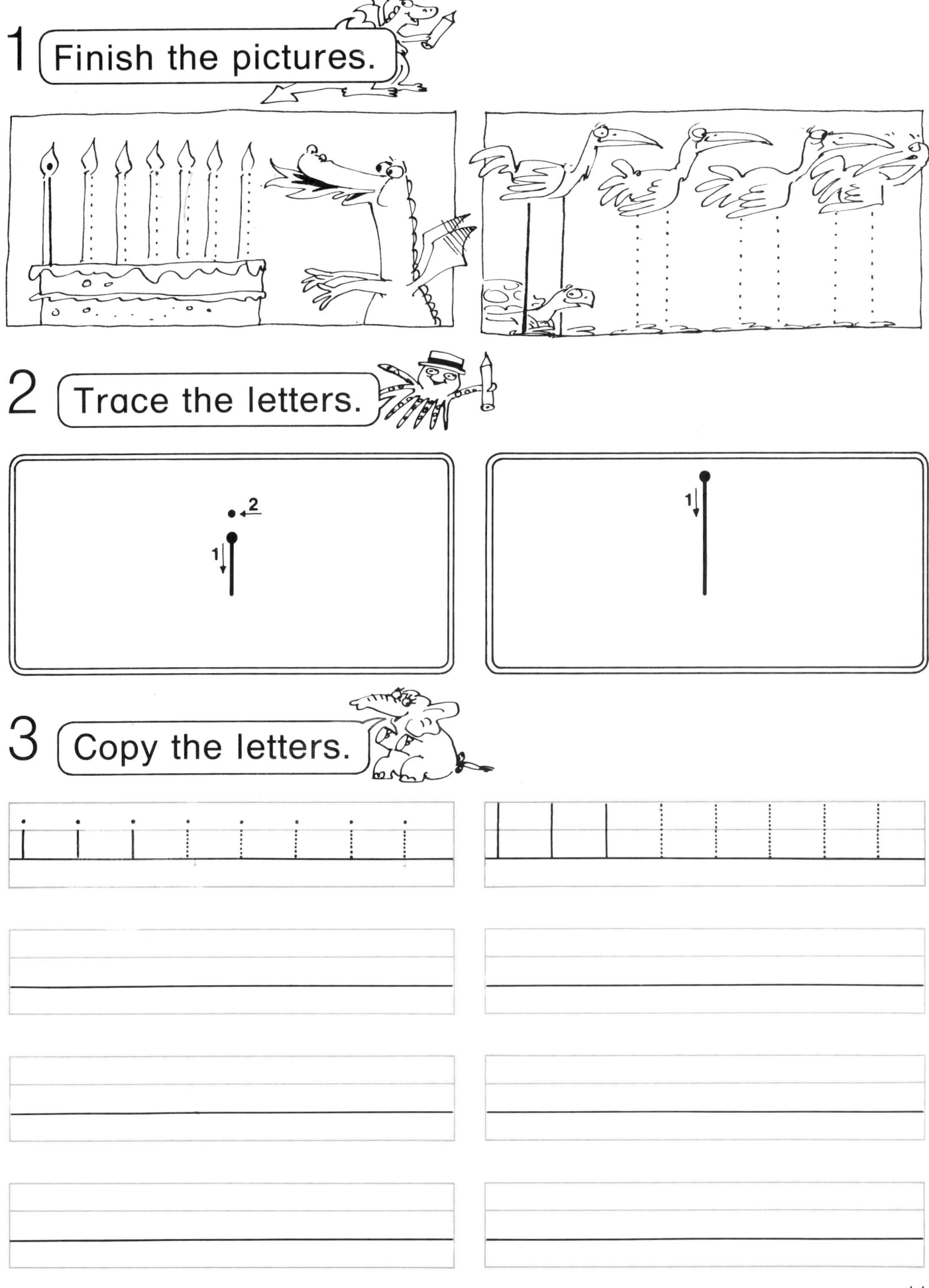

1 Finish the pictures.

2 Trace the letters.

3 Copy the letters.

1 Finish the pictures.

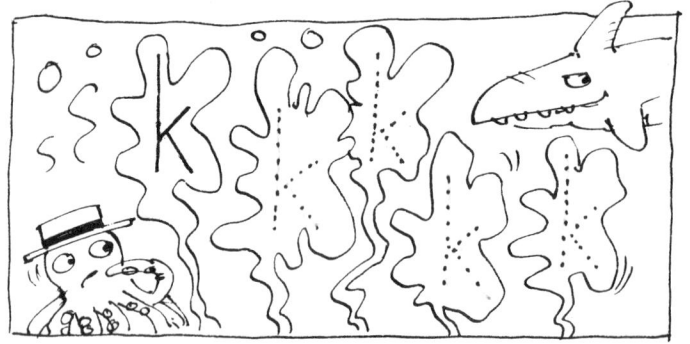

2 Trace the letters.

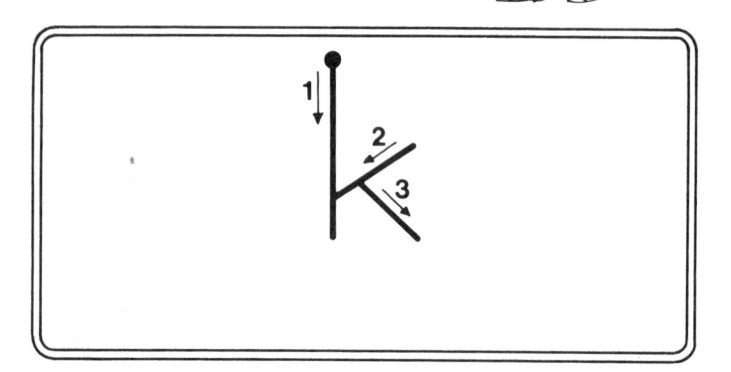

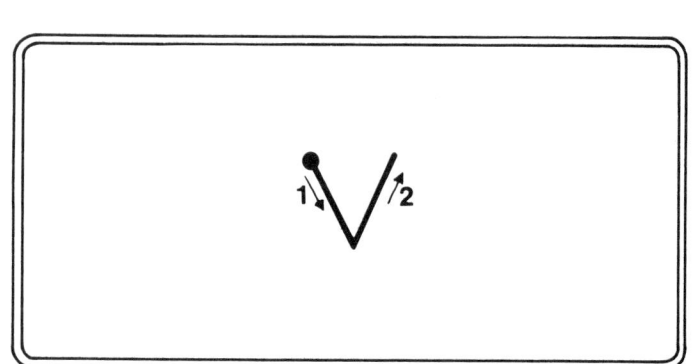

3 Copy the letters.

k k k k k k k

v v v v v v v

12

1 Finish the pictures.

2 Trace the letters.

3 Copy the letters.

W W W W W W W W

X X X X X X X X

1 Finish the picture.

2 Trace the letters.

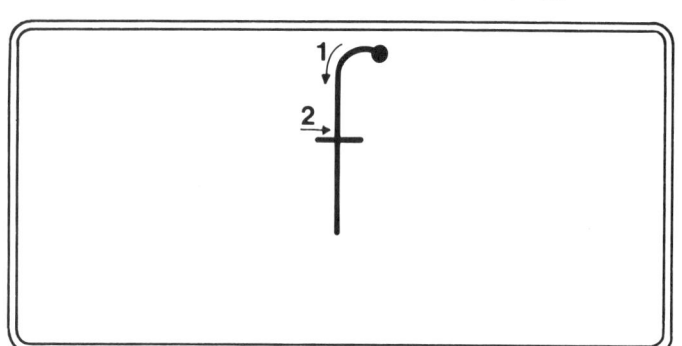

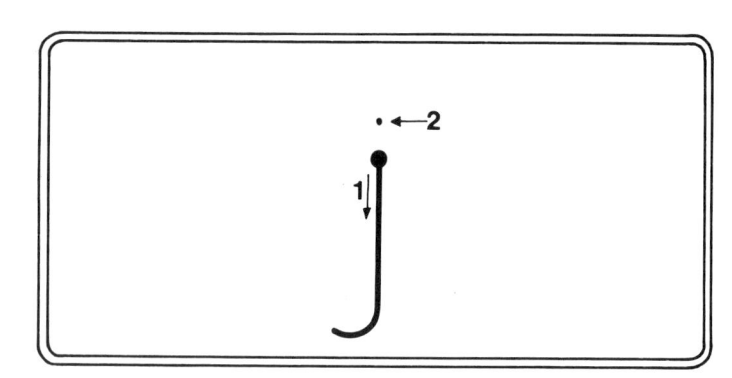

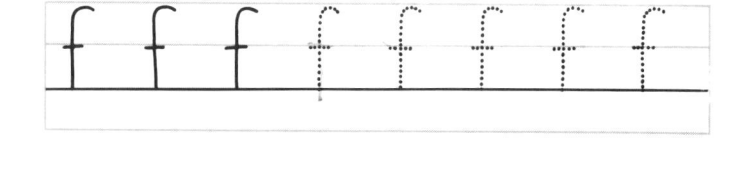

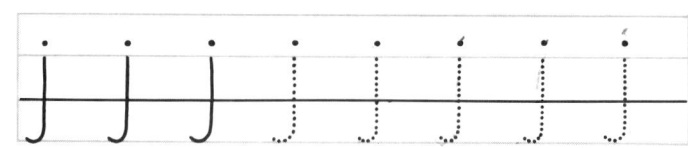

f

j

3 Copy the letters.

f f f f f f f f

j j j j j j j j

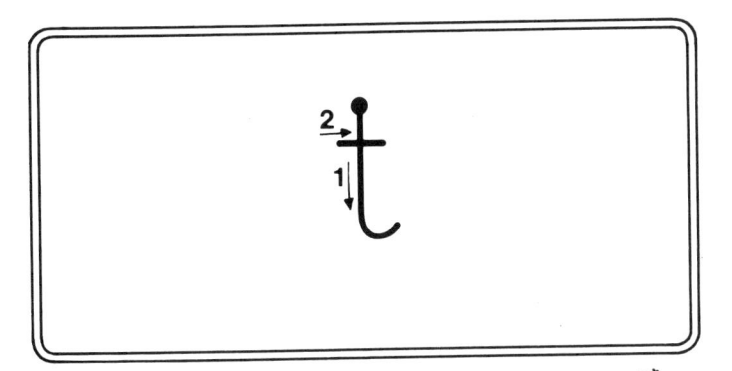

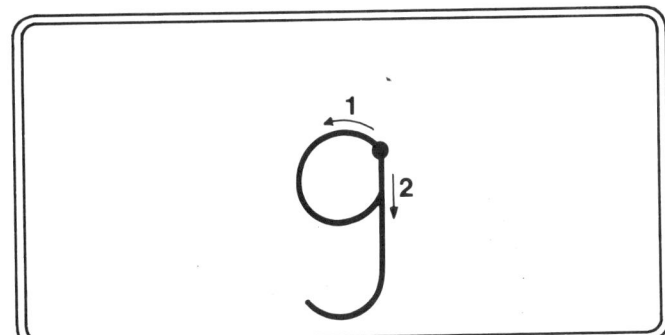

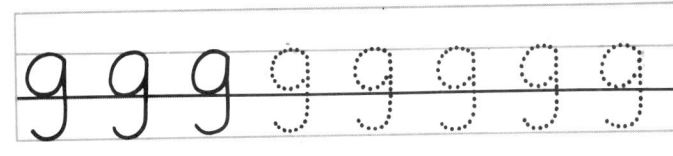

1 Finish the pictures.

2 Trace the letters.

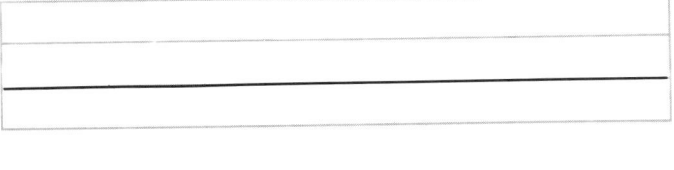

3 Copy the letters.

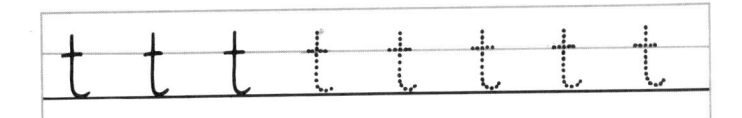

t t t t t t t t

g g g g g g g g

15

1 Finish the pictures.

2 Trace the letters.

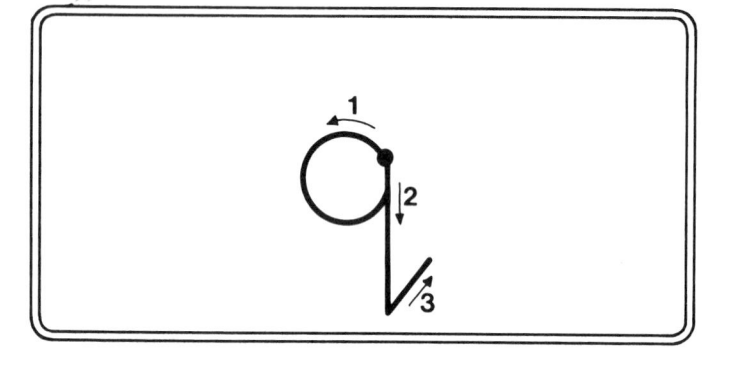

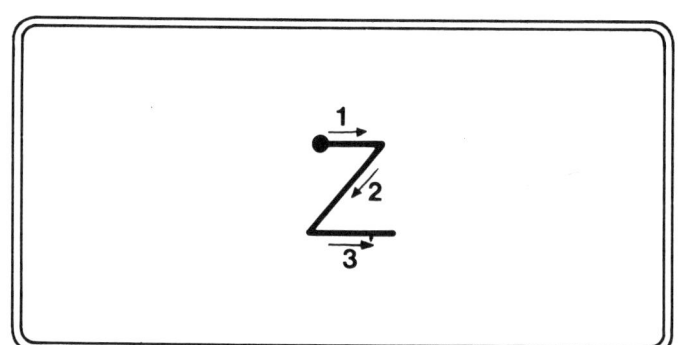

3 Copy the letters.

1. Draw a circle round the odd letter.

p	p	p	b	p	p	p	p

d	b	d	d	d	d	d	d

o	o	o	o	a	o	o	o

m	m	n	m	m	m	m	m

g	g	g	g	g	g	q	g

2. Match a letter on the right with a letter on the left. Draw a circle round the correct letter.

h	m	n	h	r	b	d	l

y	j	g	q	i	h	y	t

c	o	d	a	c	g	b	p

p	b	g	j	d	p	y	k

l	i	l	b	t	j	d	p

1 Trace the letters.

A

B

2 Copy the letters.

A A A A A A A

B B B B B B B

3 Practise the letters.

Aa Aa Aa Aa

Bb Bb Bb Bb

18

1 Trace the letters.

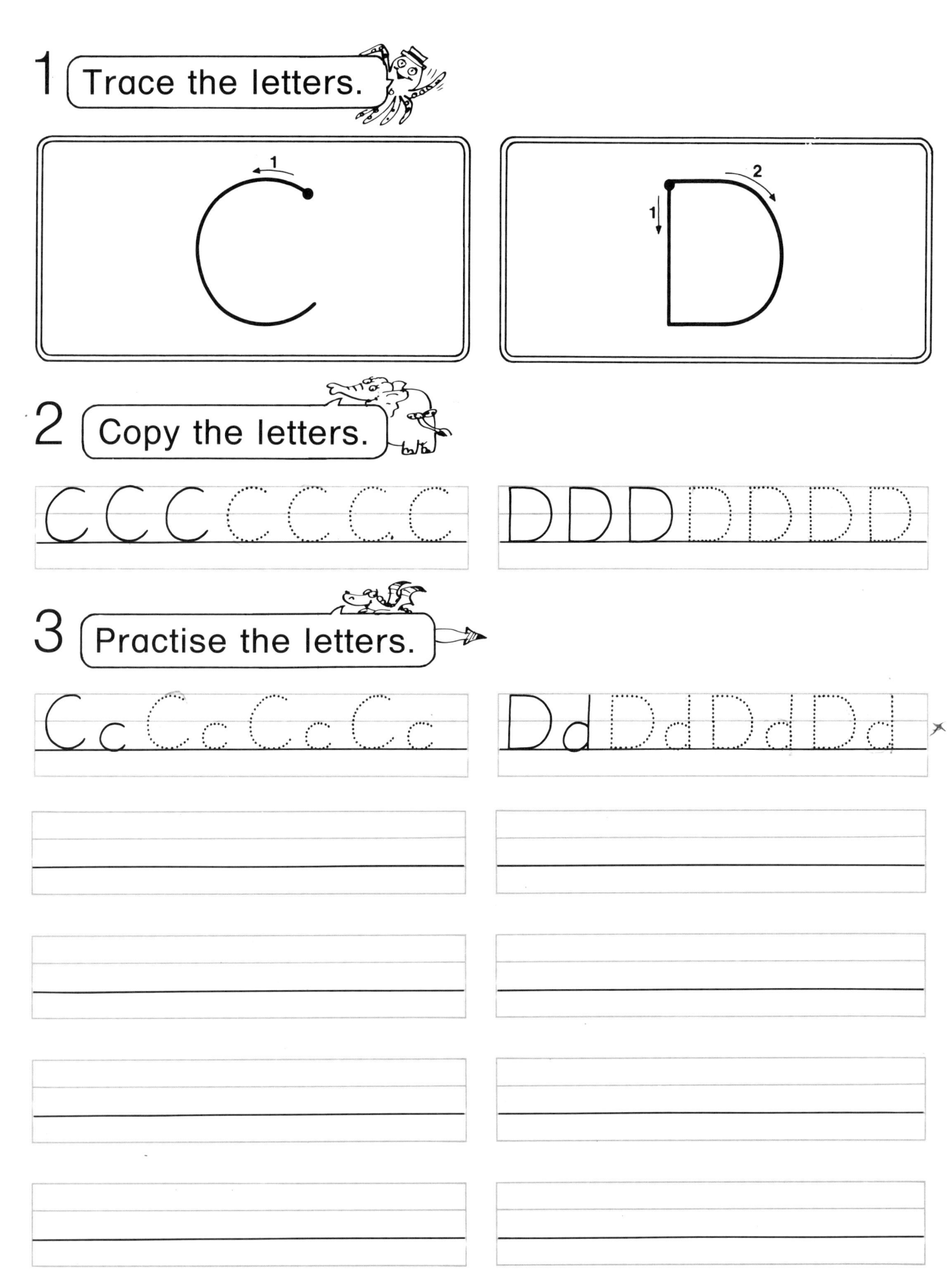

C   D

2 Copy the letters.

CCC CCCC   DDD DDDD

3 Practise the letters.

Cc Cc Cc Cc   Dd Dd Dd Dd

1 Trace the letters.

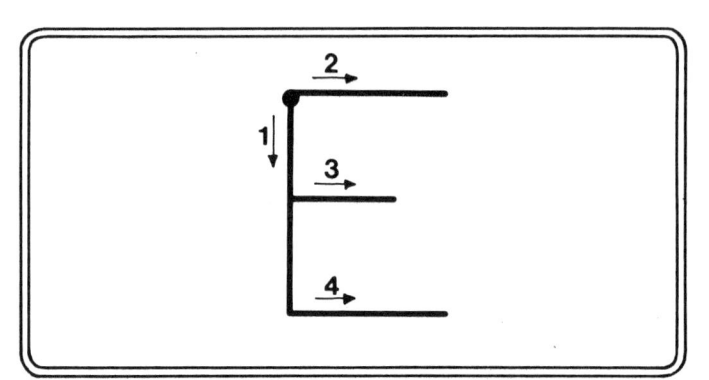

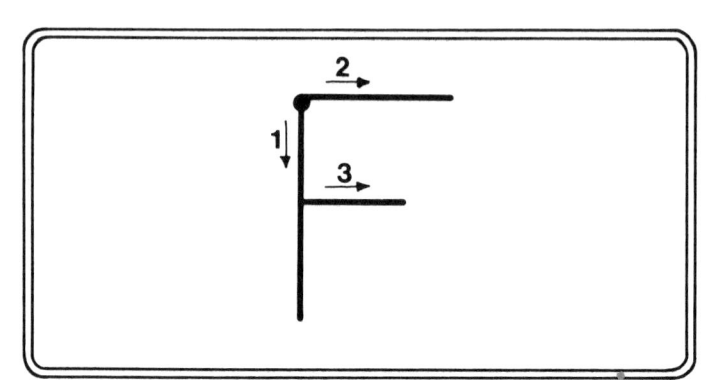

2 Copy the letters.

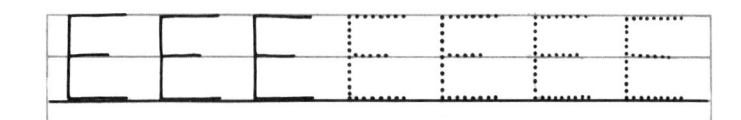

3 Practise the letters.

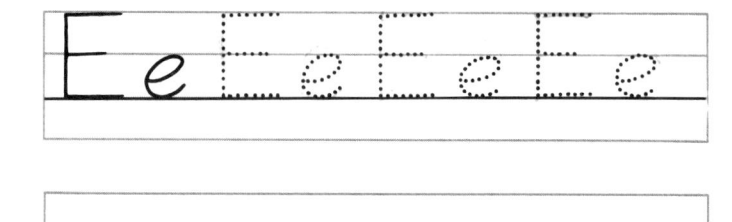

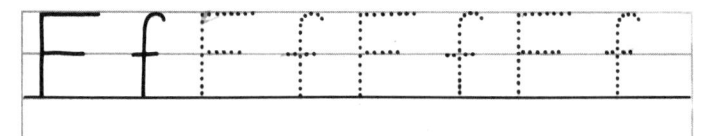

20

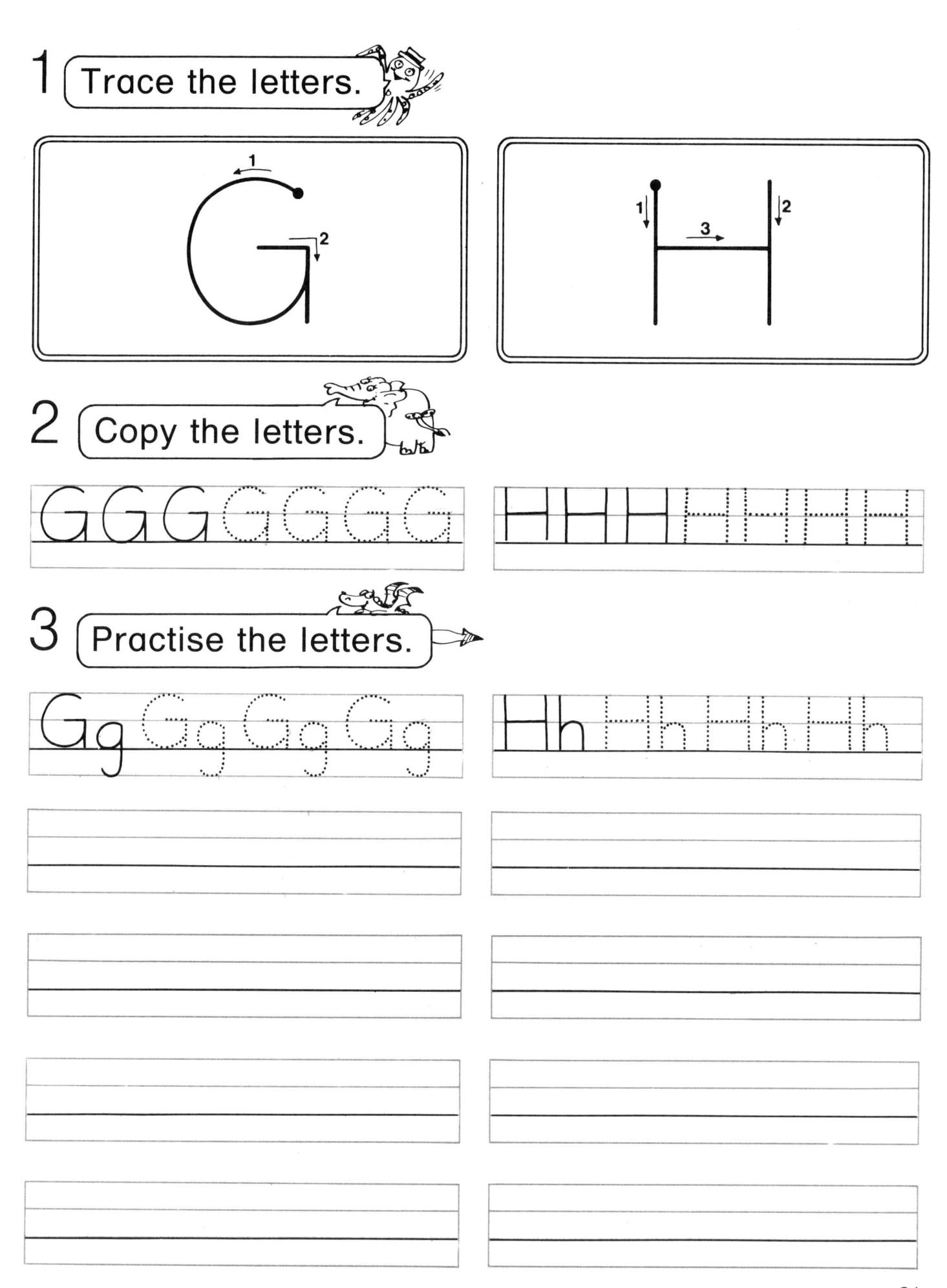

1 Trace the letters.

2 Copy the letters.

3 Practise the letters.

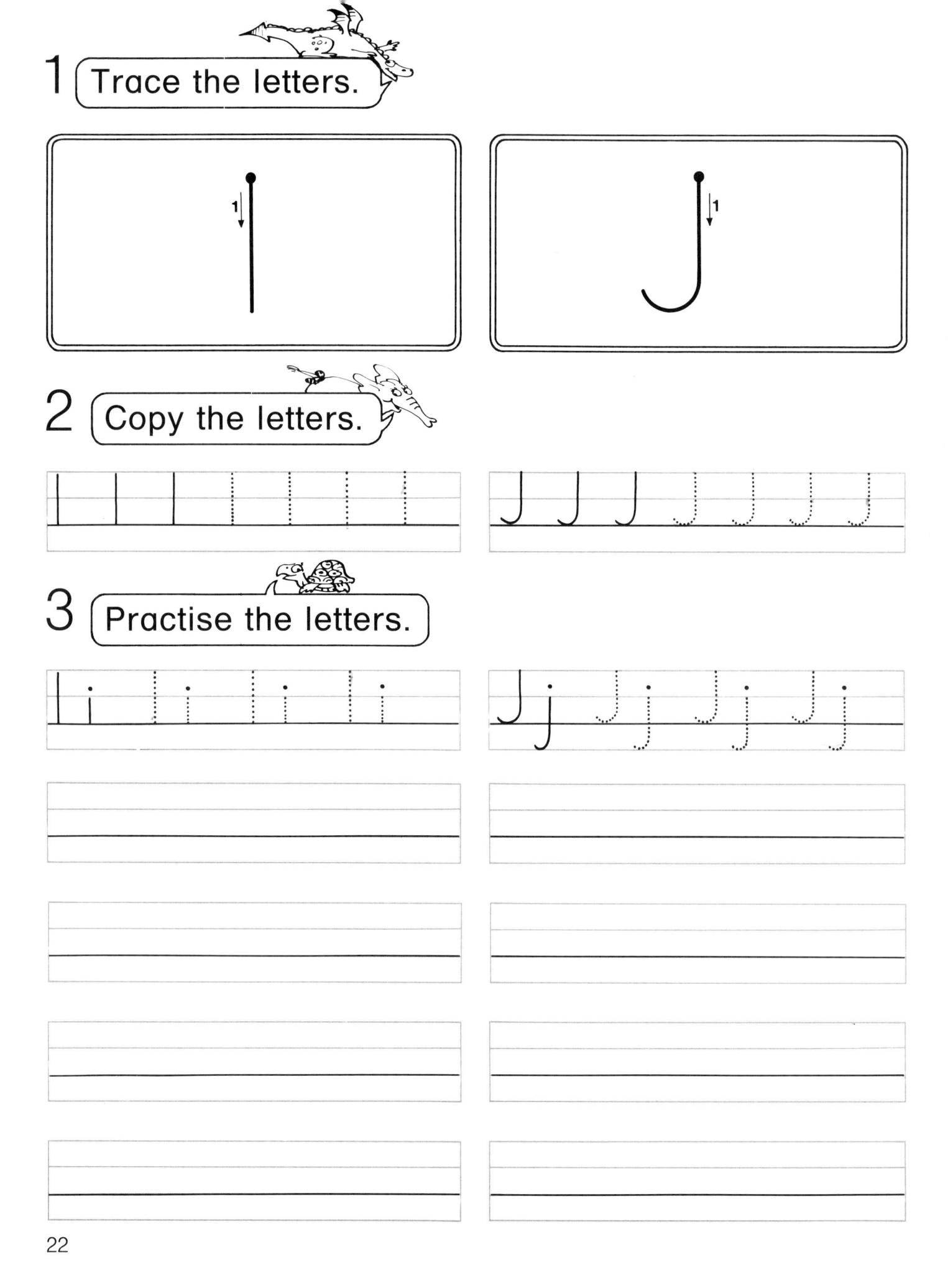

1 Trace the letters.

2 Copy the letters.

3 Practise the letters.

1 Trace the letters.

2 Copy the letters.

K K K K K K   L L L L L L L

3 Practise the letters.

Kk Kk Kk Kk   Ll Ll Ll Ll

1 Trace the letters.

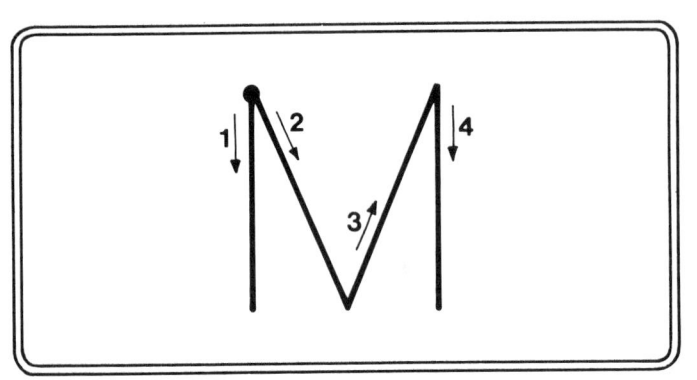

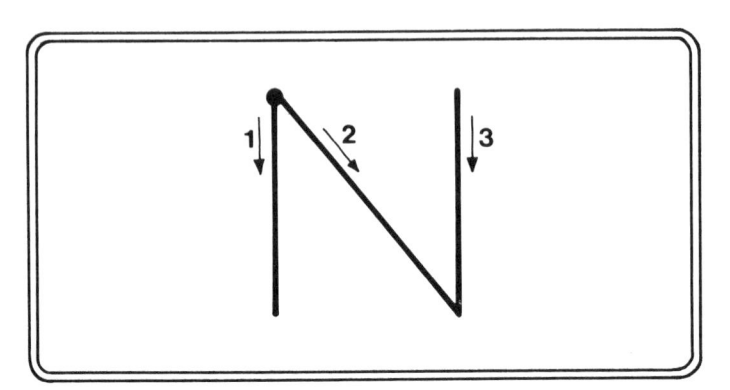

2 Copy the letters.

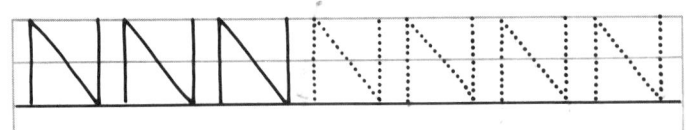

3 Practise the letters.

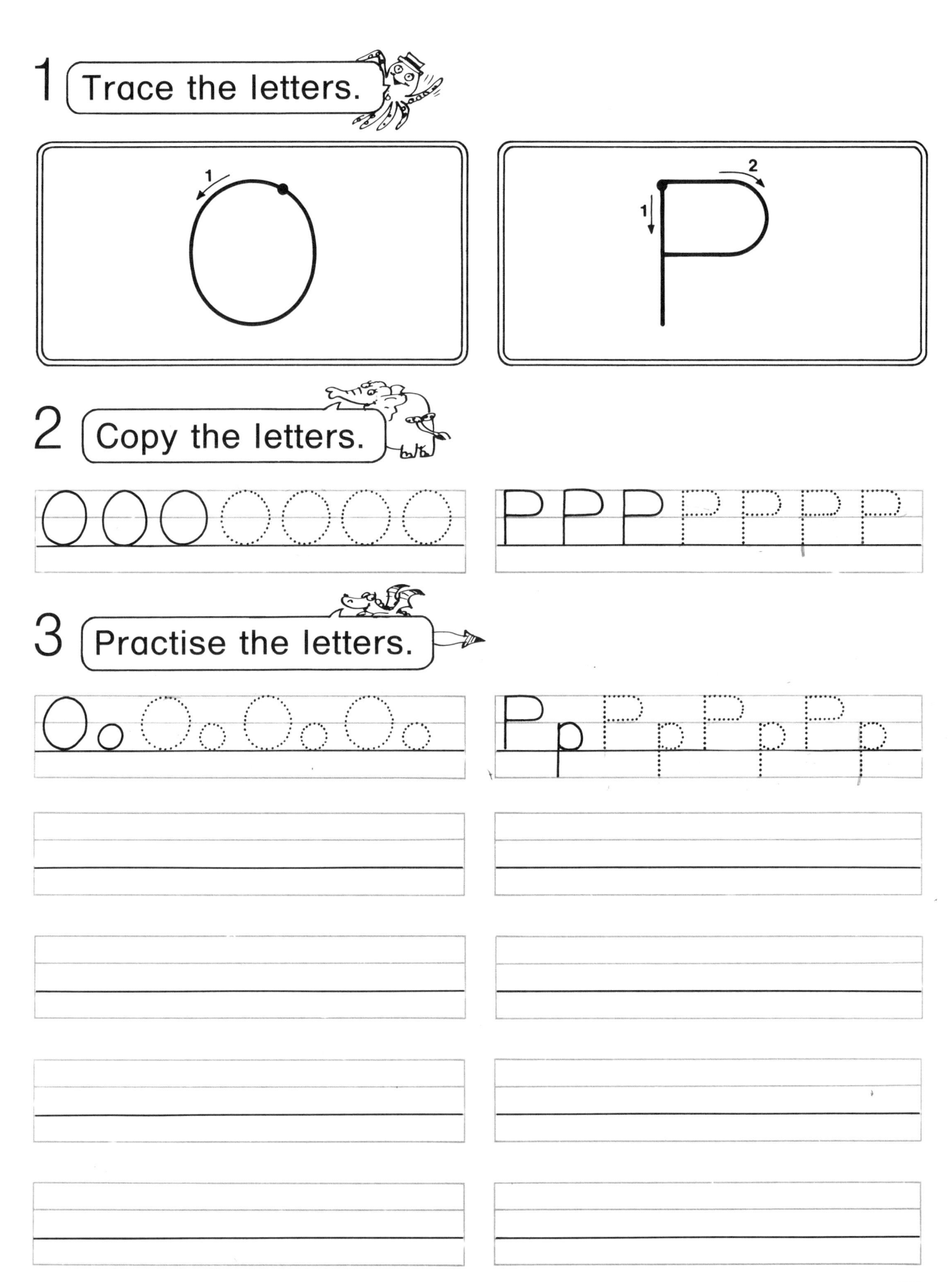

1 Trace the letters.

2 Copy the letters.

3 Practise the letters.

1 Trace the letters.

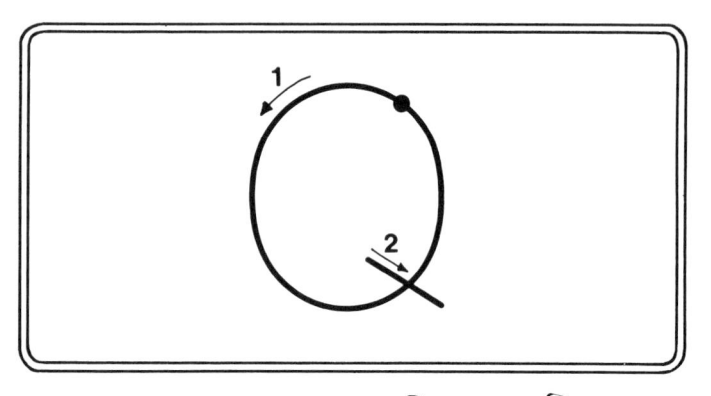

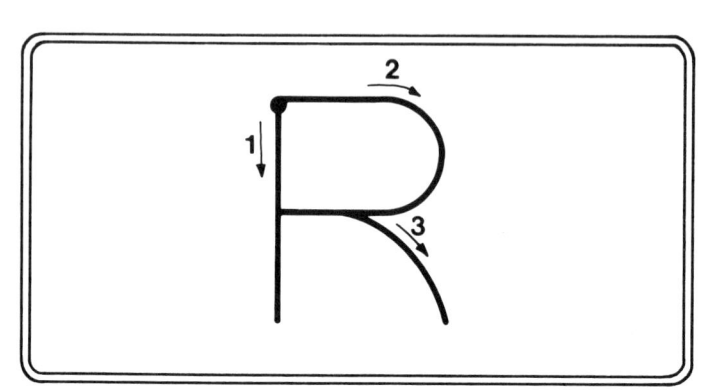

2 Copy the letters.

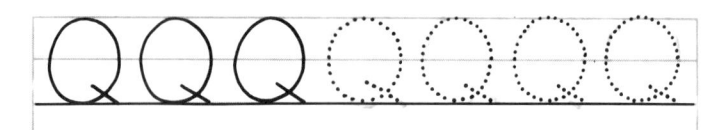

QQQ QQQ   RRR RRR

3 Practise the letters.

Qq Qq Qq Qq   Rr Rr Rr Rr

1 Trace the letters.

S

T

2 Copy the letters.

S S S S S S S

T T T T T T T

3 Practise the letters.

Ss Ss Ss Ss

Tt Tt Tt Tt

1 Trace the letters.

U   V

2 Copy the letters.

UUU UUUU   VVV VVVV

3 Practise the letters.

Uu Uu Uu Uu Uu   Vv Vv Vv Vv

1. Trace the letters.

2. Copy the letters.

3. Practise the letters.

1 Trace the letters.

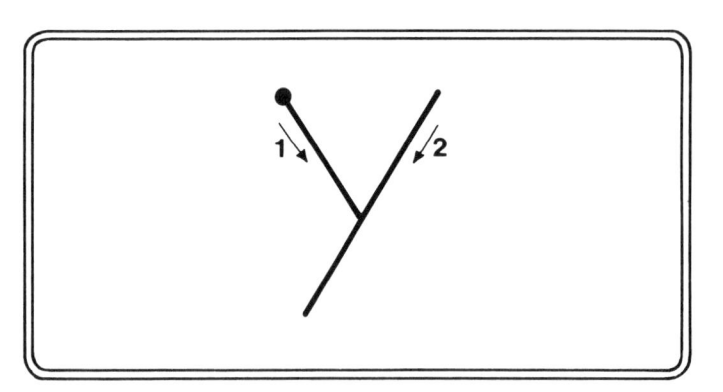

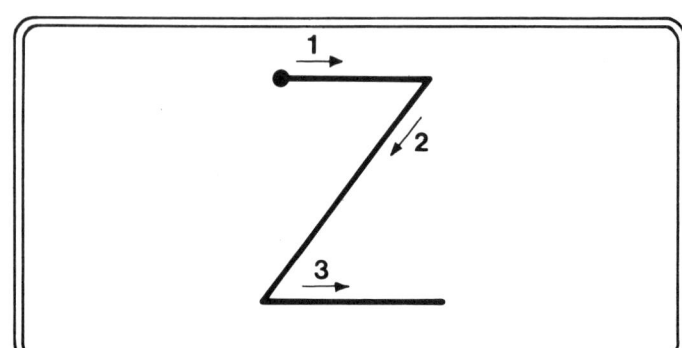

2 Copy the letters.

3 Practise the letters.

1 Copy the numbers.

1	2	3	4
3	4
2	4
5	6	7	8
5	7
6	8
9	10
9	10

1. Join the capital letters with the correct small letter.

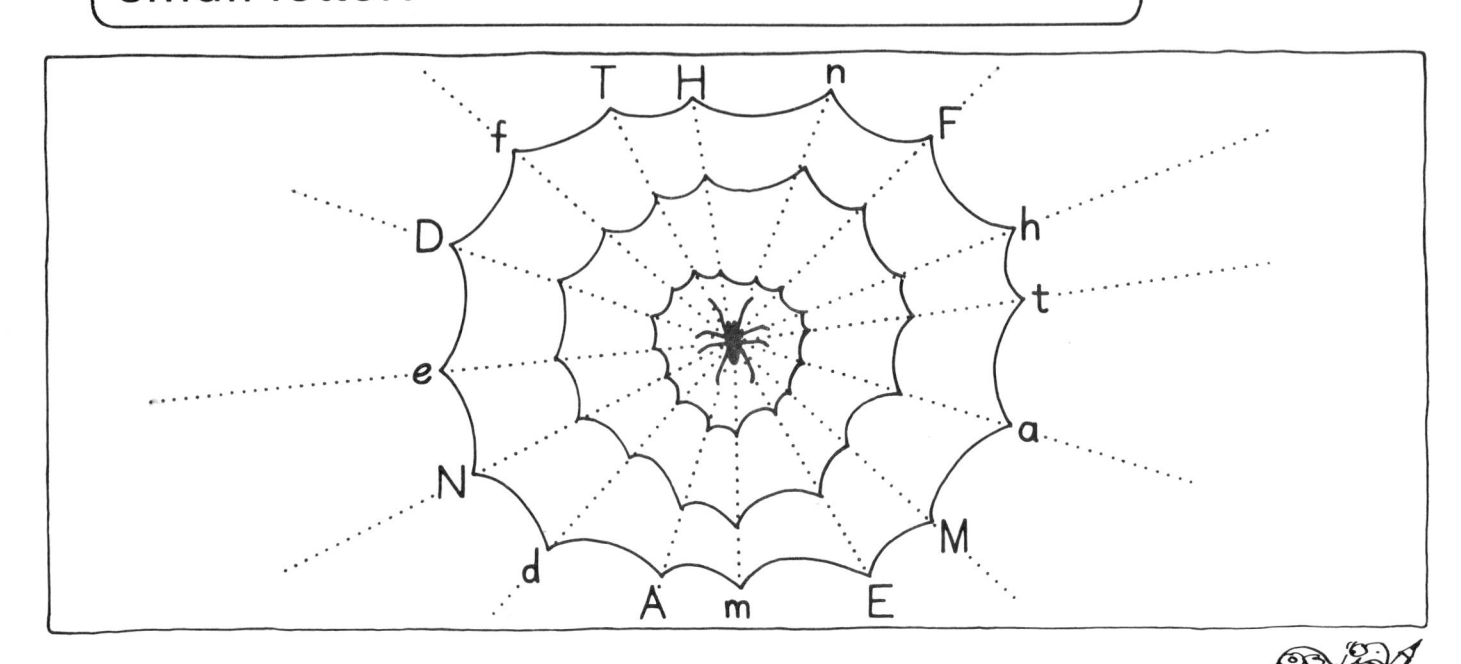

2. Match a letter on the right with a letter on the left. Draw a circle round the correct letter.

A	n	m	a	h	e
D	d	b	p	g	k
G	e	p	g	f	j
P	q	d	b	p	r
R	v	b	p	r	t
N	m	n	r	o	u